EMMANUEL JOSEPH

Economies Unshackled, The Cryptocurrency Blueprint for Global Commerce

Copyright © 2025 by Emmanuel Joseph

All rights reserved. No part of this publication may be reproduced, stored or transmitted in any form or by any means, electronic, mechanical, photocopying, recording, scanning, or otherwise without written permission from the publisher. It is illegal to copy this book, post it to a website, or distribute it by any other means without permission.

First edition

This book was professionally typeset on Reedsy. Find out more at reedsy.com

Contents

1	Chapter 1	1
2	Chapter 1: The Rise of Cryptocurrencies	3
3	Chapter 2: Blockchain Technology: The Backbone of...	5
4	Chapter 3: Decentralized Finance (DeFi): Revolutionizing...	7
5	Chapter 4: The Global Impact of Cryptocurrencies	9
6	Chapter 5: Cryptocurrencies and Financial Inclusion	11
7	Chapter 6: The Regulatory Landscape	13
8	Chapter 7: Environmental Concerns and Sustainable Solutions	15
9	Chapter 8: Cryptocurrencies in E-Commerce	17
10	Chapter 9: Tokenization and the New Digital Economy	19
11	Chapter 10: Cryptocurrencies and Central Bank Digital...	21
12	Chapter 11: Cryptocurrencies and the Future of Work	23
13	Chapter 12: The Road Ahead	25

1

Chapter 1

Introduction

In the ever-evolving landscape of global finance, cryptocurrencies have emerged as a revolutionary force, challenging the very foundations of traditional economic systems. Born out of the desire for greater financial autonomy and transparency, cryptocurrencies have rapidly evolved from a niche innovation into a formidable asset class with the potential to reshape global commerce. As we navigate the complexities and opportunities presented by this digital revolution, it becomes increasingly clear that cryptocurrencies are more than just a speculative investment—they represent a blueprint for a new era of economic freedom and inclusivity.

"Economies Unshackled: The Cryptocurrency Blueprint for Global Commerce" delves into the transformative power of digital currencies and blockchain technology. This book explores the origins and evolution of cryptocurrencies, tracing their journey from the early days of Bitcoin to the rise of decentralized finance (DeFi) and central bank digital currencies (CBDCs). Through a comprehensive analysis of the key innovations, challenges, and opportunities in the crypto space, this book aims to provide readers with a deeper understanding of the potential impact of cryptocurrencies on the global economy.

At the heart of this exploration lies the promise of financial inclusion and empowerment. Cryptocurrencies have the potential to democratize access to financial services, bridging the gap between the banked and unbanked populations. They offer new opportunities for wealth creation and economic participation, particularly in regions where traditional banking infrastructure is lacking. By eliminating intermediaries and reducing transaction costs, cryptocurrencies can foster greater efficiency and transparency in financial transactions, paving the way for a more equitable and resilient global financial system.

As we embark on this journey through the world of cryptocurrencies, "Economies Unshackled" invites readers to envision a future where economic barriers are dismantled, and financial opportunities are accessible to all. This book serves as a guide to understanding the transformative potential of digital currencies and provides a roadmap for harnessing their power to create a more inclusive and prosperous global economy. Together, let's explore the blueprint for a new era of global commerce, unshackled from the limitations of traditional financial systems.

2

Chapter 1: The Rise of Cryptocurrencies

The genesis of cryptocurrencies can be traced back to the aftermath of the global financial crisis of 2008. This era of economic turmoil exposed the vulnerabilities and inefficiencies inherent in traditional financial systems, setting the stage for an alternative form of currency that operates independently of centralized control. Bitcoin, introduced by the pseudonymous Satoshi Nakamoto in 2009, marked the dawn of this new financial era. Cryptocurrencies promised transparency, security, and decentralized governance, addressing the shortcomings that had plagued conventional banking systems for decades.

As Bitcoin gained traction, it inspired the creation of numerous other cryptocurrencies, each aiming to solve specific financial challenges. Ethereum, introduced in 2015 by Vitalik Buterin, revolutionized the space by enabling smart contracts—self-executing contracts with the terms of the agreement directly written into code. This innovation expanded the potential applications of blockchain technology beyond mere currency and laid the groundwork for decentralized finance (DeFi) and non-fungible tokens (NFTs). The proliferation of these digital assets signaled a paradigm shift in the way value is stored and transferred.

Despite initial skepticism and regulatory hurdles, cryptocurrencies gradually gained acceptance among mainstream investors and institutions. The appeal of a decentralized financial system, immune to the whims of central banks and governments, resonated with a growing number of individuals and organizations. Major financial institutions began to explore blockchain technology, recognizing its potential to enhance efficiency and reduce costs. By the late 2010s, cryptocurrencies had evolved from a niche interest into a formidable force in the global financial landscape.

The rapid evolution of the cryptocurrency market also brought challenges, particularly in terms of regulation and security. High-profile incidents of hacking and fraud underscored the need for robust security measures and regulatory frameworks. Governments around the world grappled with the task of balancing innovation with consumer protection. As the market matured, it became evident that the future of cryptocurrencies would hinge on their ability to integrate seamlessly with existing financial systems while maintaining the core principles of decentralization and transparency.

3

Chapter 2: Blockchain Technology: The Backbone of Cryptocurrencies

Blockchain technology, the foundational innovation underpinning cryptocurrencies, is a decentralized ledger that records transactions across a network of computers. This structure ensures that each transaction is transparent, immutable, and secure. Unlike traditional databases, a blockchain is resistant to tampering and fraud, as altering any part of the chain would require consensus from the majority of the network's participants. This inherent security has made blockchain a vital tool in the quest for more reliable and efficient financial systems.

The concept of a blockchain is relatively simple, yet its implications are profound. Each block in the chain contains a list of transactions, and once a block is added to the chain, it cannot be changed without altering all subsequent blocks. This feature provides a transparent and verifiable record of all transactions, which can be audited by anyone. This transparency builds trust among participants, eliminating the need for intermediaries such as banks or clearinghouses, and reducing transaction costs and times.

Blockchain's potential extends far beyond cryptocurrencies. In supply chain management, for example, blockchain can be used to trace the origin and movement of goods, ensuring authenticity and reducing fraud. In the healthcare sector, blockchain can provide secure and verifiable patient records, enhancing privacy and improving the accuracy of medical information. The technology's applications are virtually limitless, and its adoption is poised to disrupt numerous industries by introducing new levels of efficiency, security, and transparency.

However, the widespread adoption of blockchain technology is not without its challenges. Scalability remains a significant concern, as the current infrastructure struggles to handle large volumes of transactions quickly and efficiently. Additionally, the energy consumption associated with blockchain networks, particularly proof-of-work systems like Bitcoin, has raised environmental concerns. Despite these hurdles, ongoing research and development efforts are focused on creating more scalable and sustainable blockchain solutions, ensuring that this transformative technology can be harnessed to its full potential.

4

Chapter 3: Decentralized Finance (DeFi): Revolutionizing Traditional Banking

Decentralized finance, or DeFi, represents a fundamental shift in the way financial services are delivered. By leveraging blockchain technology, DeFi platforms eliminate the need for traditional financial intermediaries, such as banks and brokers, enabling users to access a wide range of financial services directly. These services include lending, borrowing, trading, and earning interest, all conducted in a decentralized manner. This democratization of finance has the potential to increase financial inclusion and empower individuals who have been underserved by the traditional banking system.

One of the key innovations in the DeFi space is the use of smart contracts, which automate and enforce the terms of financial agreements without the need for intermediaries. These self-executing contracts ensure that transactions are secure and transparent, reducing the risk of fraud and increasing efficiency. For example, DeFi lending platforms allow users to lend their assets to others in exchange for interest, with the entire process governed by smart contracts. This not only provides users with passive income opportunities but also offers borrowers access to capital without the need for credit checks or collateral requirements imposed by traditional banks.

The growth of DeFi has also spurred the development of decentralized exchanges (DEXs), which enable users to trade cryptocurrencies directly with one another without relying on a centralized exchange. DEXs offer several advantages, including increased security, as users retain control of their assets throughout the trading process, and reduced risk of hacking, as there is no central point of failure. Additionally, DEXs promote transparency, as all transactions are recorded on the blockchain and can be audited by anyone. The rise of DEXs has contributed to the overall liquidity and efficiency of the cryptocurrency market.

Despite its rapid growth and potential, the DeFi ecosystem faces several challenges. Regulatory uncertainty remains a significant hurdle, as governments around the world grapple with how to oversee and regulate these new financial systems. Security concerns also persist, as smart contract vulnerabilities and hacking incidents continue to pose risks. Moreover, the complexity of DeFi platforms can be a barrier to entry for mainstream users, who may find it difficult to navigate and understand these new technologies. Nevertheless, the ongoing development and refinement of DeFi solutions hold promise for a more inclusive and resilient financial future.

5

Chapter 4: The Global Impact of Cryptocurrencies

The rise of cryptocurrencies has had far-reaching implications for the global economy. By providing an alternative to traditional financial systems, cryptocurrencies have introduced a new level of financial freedom and autonomy for individuals and businesses. In regions with unstable currencies or limited access to banking services, cryptocurrencies offer a lifeline, enabling people to store and transfer value securely and efficiently. This has the potential to drive economic growth and development in underserved areas, fostering greater financial inclusion and reducing poverty.

In addition to their impact on individuals, cryptocurrencies have also disrupted traditional industries and business models. For example, the remittance industry, which facilitates cross-border money transfers, has been significantly affected by the rise of cryptocurrencies. Traditional remittance services often charge high fees and take several days to process transactions, whereas cryptocurrency-based remittances can be completed almost instantaneously and at a fraction of the cost. This has made it easier and more affordable for people to send money to their families and communities, particularly in developing countries.

The global adoption of cryptocurrencies has also spurred innovation and investment in blockchain technology. As businesses and governments explore the potential applications of blockchain, new use cases and industries are emerging. From supply chain management and healthcare to real estate and entertainment, blockchain technology is poised to revolutionize a wide range of sectors. This wave of innovation has attracted significant investment from venture capital firms and institutional investors, driving further research and development in the space.

However, the global impact of cryptocurrencies is not without its challenges. Regulatory frameworks vary widely between countries, creating a fragmented landscape that can be difficult to navigate for businesses and investors. Additionally, the environmental concerns associated with cryptocurrency mining have sparked debates about the sustainability of the industry. As the world grapples with these challenges, it will be crucial to find a balance between fostering innovation and ensuring responsible and sustainable growth.

6

Chapter 5: Cryptocurrencies and Financial Inclusion

One of the most compelling aspects of cryptocurrencies is their potential to promote financial inclusion. Around the world, billions of people remain unbanked or underbanked, lacking access to essential financial services. Cryptocurrencies can bridge this gap by providing a decentralized and accessible alternative to traditional banking. With just a smartphone and an internet connection, individuals can participate in the global economy, access financial services, and build wealth.

In many developing countries, the traditional banking infrastructure is either inadequate or nonexistent. Cryptocurrencies offer a solution by enabling peer-to-peer transactions without the need for intermediaries. This can significantly reduce transaction costs and make financial services more affordable for low-income individuals. Moreover, cryptocurrencies can facilitate cross-border remittances, allowing people to send money to their families and communities without incurring high fees. This has the potential to uplift entire communities and drive economic development.

Additionally, cryptocurrencies can empower small businesses and entrepreneurs by providing them with access to capital and financial services. Traditional banking systems often impose stringent requirements for loans and credit, making it difficult for small businesses to grow and thrive.

Cryptocurrencies, on the other hand, enable businesses to raise funds through decentralized platforms, such as initial coin offerings (ICOs) and decentralized finance (DeFi) lending. This democratization of finance can spur innovation and create new economic opportunities.

However, the promise of financial inclusion through cryptocurrencies is not without challenges. Digital literacy and access to technology remain significant barriers in many regions. Education and outreach efforts are essential to ensure that individuals can safely and effectively use cryptocurrencies. Additionally, regulatory uncertainty and the volatility of cryptocurrency markets pose risks that need to be addressed. Despite these challenges, the potential of cryptocurrencies to promote financial inclusion remains a powerful force for positive change.

7

Chapter 6: The Regulatory Landscape

As cryptocurrencies have gained prominence, governments and regulatory bodies around the world have grappled with how to oversee and regulate this new financial frontier. The regulatory landscape for cryptocurrencies is diverse, with different countries adopting varying approaches. Some nations have embraced cryptocurrencies and blockchain technology, creating favorable regulatory environments to foster innovation. Others have taken a more cautious approach, imposing strict regulations or even outright bans to mitigate risks.

In countries that have adopted a proactive stance towards cryptocurrencies, regulatory frameworks aim to balance innovation with consumer protection. For example, Switzerland has established itself as a global hub for blockchain and cryptocurrency startups, offering clear guidelines and supportive regulations. Similarly, Singapore has implemented a regulatory sandbox to encourage experimentation while ensuring that risks are managed. These approaches have attracted significant investment and talent, positioning these countries as leaders in the crypto space.

On the other hand, some countries have expressed concerns about the potential risks associated with cryptocurrencies, such as money laundering, tax evasion, and financial instability. China, for example, has imposed stringent regulations on cryptocurrency trading and mining, citing concerns about financial stability and environmental impact. India has also grappled with regulatory uncertainty, with the government considering various approaches to regulate the crypto market. These measures reflect the challenges that regulators face in balancing the benefits of innovation with the need to protect consumers and maintain financial stability.

International cooperation is crucial to addressing the regulatory challenges posed by cryptocurrencies. As digital assets transcend national borders, harmonized regulatory frameworks can help prevent regulatory arbitrage and promote a more stable and secure global financial system. Organizations such as the Financial Action Task Force (FATF) and the International Monetary Fund (IMF) have called for international standards and cooperation to address the risks and opportunities presented by cryptocurrencies. As the regulatory landscape continues to evolve, finding the right balance between innovation and oversight will be key to unlocking the full potential of cryptocurrencies.

8

Chapter 7: Environmental Concerns and Sustainable Solutions

The environmental impact of cryptocurrency mining has been a topic of intense debate and scrutiny. The process of mining, particularly for proof-of-work (PoW) cryptocurrencies like Bitcoin, requires significant computational power and energy consumption. This has raised concerns about the sustainability of the industry, especially in light of global efforts to combat climate change and reduce carbon emissions.

Bitcoin mining, for example, involves solving complex mathematical problems to validate transactions and secure the network. This process consumes vast amounts of electricity, often from non-renewable sources. As a result, the carbon footprint of Bitcoin mining has drawn criticism from environmental advocates and policymakers. Addressing these concerns is crucial to ensuring the long-term viability and acceptance of cryptocurrencies.

In response to environmental concerns, the cryptocurrency industry has explored various sustainable solutions. One approach is the transition to more energy-efficient consensus mechanisms, such as proof-of-stake (PoS). Unlike PoW, PoS does not rely on intensive computational work to validate transactions. Instead, validators are chosen based on the number of coins they hold and are willing to "stake" as collateral. This significantly reduces energy consumption and carbon emissions, making it a more sustainable option. Ethereum's transition from PoW to PoS, known as Ethereum 2.0, is a prominent example of this shift towards sustainability.

Another solution is the adoption of renewable energy sources for mining operations. Some mining companies have begun to establish facilities in regions with abundant renewable energy, such as hydropower, solar, and wind. By tapping into cleaner energy sources, the environmental impact of cryptocurrency mining can be mitigated. Additionally, innovations in mining hardware and techniques continue to improve energy efficiency, further reducing the industry's carbon footprint.

The environmental challenges associated with cryptocurrencies underscore the importance of sustainable practices and innovation. As the industry evolves, it will be essential to prioritize environmental considerations alongside technological advancements. By embracing sustainable solutions, the cryptocurrency ecosystem can contribute to a greener future while continuing to drive financial innovation.

9

Chapter 8: Cryptocurrencies in E-Commerce

The integration of cryptocurrencies into e-commerce has opened up new possibilities for global commerce. By offering an alternative to traditional payment methods, cryptocurrencies enable faster, cheaper, and more secure transactions. This has the potential to revolutionize the e-commerce landscape, providing benefits for both merchants and consumers.

One of the primary advantages of using cryptocurrencies in e-commerce is the reduction in transaction costs. Traditional payment methods, such as credit cards and bank transfers, often involve significant fees for processing payments and currency conversion. Cryptocurrencies, on the other hand, allow for near-instantaneous cross-border transactions with minimal fees. This is particularly advantageous for small businesses and international merchants, who can save on costs and pass on the benefits to their customers.

Moreover, cryptocurrencies offer enhanced security for online transactions. Traditional payment methods are susceptible to fraud and chargebacks, which can be costly and time-consuming for merchants to resolve. Cryptocurrencies utilize blockchain technology to create a secure and transparent record of transactions, reducing the risk of fraud and providing greater peace of mind for both buyers and sellers. Additionally, the use of cryptocurrencies can protect sensitive financial information, as transactions do not require the sharing of personal or credit card details.

The adoption of cryptocurrencies in e-commerce is still in its early stages, but several major companies have already begun to accept digital currencies as a form of payment. This trend is expected to continue as more businesses recognize the benefits and consumer demand for cryptocurrency payment options grows. However, challenges remain, such as regulatory uncertainty and the volatility of cryptocurrency prices. Addressing these issues will be crucial to the widespread adoption of cryptocurrencies in the e-commerce sector.

10

Chapter 9: Tokenization and the New Digital Economy

Tokenization is the process of converting assets into digital tokens that can be traded on a blockchain. This innovation has the potential to transform the way we think about ownership and value, creating new opportunities for investment and commerce. By representing physical and digital assets as tokens, blockchain technology can increase liquidity, reduce transaction costs, and enhance transparency.

One of the most promising applications of tokenization is in the real estate market. Traditionally, real estate investments have been illiquid and inaccessible to many investors due to high entry costs and complex legal processes. Tokenizing real estate allows for fractional ownership, enabling investors to buy and sell shares in a property with ease. This democratization of real estate investment can increase market liquidity and provide new opportunities for diversification.

In addition to real estate, tokenization can be applied to a wide range of assets, including art, commodities, and intellectual property. For example, artists can tokenize their work and sell shares to collectors, allowing them to retain ownership while raising funds. Similarly, companies can tokenize their intellectual property, such as patents and trademarks, to raise capital and facilitate licensing agreements. The ability to trade tokens on decentralized platforms further enhances the accessibility and efficiency of these markets.

The rise of tokenization is also giving birth to a new digital economy, characterized by the seamless exchange of value across borders and platforms. This digital economy is powered by decentralized applications (dApps) that run on blockchain networks, providing users with a wide range of services, from finance and gaming to social media and supply chain management. The proliferation of dApps is driving innovation and competition, creating a dynamic and interconnected ecosystem that is reshaping the way we interact with digital assets.

11

Chapter 10: Cryptocurrencies and Central Bank Digital Currencies (CBDCs)

The rise of cryptocurrencies has prompted central banks around the world to explore the concept of central bank digital currencies (CBDCs). Unlike cryptocurrencies, which are decentralized and operate independently of governments, CBDCs are digital versions of a country's fiat currency, issued and regulated by the central bank. The development of CBDCs reflects the growing recognition of the potential benefits of digital currencies, while addressing some of the concerns associated with cryptocurrencies.

One of the primary motivations for central banks to develop CBDCs is to improve the efficiency and security of the payment system. CBDCs can enable faster and cheaper transactions, both domestically and internationally, reducing reliance on traditional banking infrastructure. Additionally, CBDCs can enhance financial inclusion by providing a secure and accessible digital payment option for unbanked and underbanked populations. By leveraging blockchain technology, CBDCs can also provide greater transparency and traceability in the financial system.

Several countries have already made significant progress in developing and piloting CBDCs. For example, China has launched the digital yuan, also known as the Digital Currency Electronic Payment (DCEP), which is currently being tested in several cities. The Bahamas has introduced the Sand Dollar, the world's first fully operational CBDC. Other countries, such as Sweden, the United States, and the European Union, are actively researching and developing their own digital currencies. These initiatives reflect the growing interest in CBDCs as a means to modernize the financial system and enhance monetary policy.

The coexistence of cryptocurrencies and CBDCs presents both opportunities and challenges. While CBDCs can offer the stability and regulatory oversight of traditional fiat currencies, cryptocurrencies provide the benefits of decentralization and innovation. The integration of CBDCs and cryptocurrencies into the global financial system will require careful consideration of regulatory frameworks, technological infrastructure, and user adoption. Ultimately, the successful implementation of CBDCs and the continued growth of cryptocurrencies will depend on striking the right balance between innovation and stability.

12

Chapter 11: Cryptocurrencies and the Future of Work

The rise of cryptocurrencies is also reshaping the future of work, offering new opportunities for earning, investing, and creating value. The gig economy, which has already transformed traditional employment models, is further evolving with the integration of cryptocurrencies. Freelancers, remote workers, and digital nomads can now receive payments in cryptocurrencies, providing greater flexibility and access to global markets.

One of the key benefits of using cryptocurrencies for payments in the gig economy is the elimination of intermediaries and associated fees. Traditional payment methods often involve high transaction costs and delays, particularly for cross-border payments. Cryptocurrencies enable near-instantaneous transactions with minimal fees, allowing workers to receive their earnings quickly and efficiently. This is especially advantageous for freelancers and remote workers who rely on timely payments for their livelihood.

In addition to payments, cryptocurrencies are creating new opportunities for earning income through decentralized platforms. For example, decentralized finance (DeFi) platforms allow individuals to lend their assets and earn interest, participate in yield farming, and engage in decentralized trading. Similarly, blockchain-based marketplaces enable creators to tokenize and sell their digital content, such as artwork, music, and writing, directly to consumers. These platforms provide greater control and ownership over one's work, fostering a more inclusive and equitable economy.

The future of work is also being influenced by the rise of decentralized autonomous organizations (DAOs). DAOs are organizations governed by smart contracts, with decisions made collectively by token holders. This decentralized governance model enables more democratic and transparent decision-making processes, empowering individuals to participate in the management and direction of projects. DAOs have the potential to disrupt traditional corporate structures, creating new opportunities for collaboration and innovation.

13

Chapter 12: The Road Ahead

As we look to the future, the potential of cryptocurrencies to transform global commerce and finance is vast. The journey of cryptocurrencies from a niche interest to a mainstream force has been marked by innovation, challenges, and resilience. As the ecosystem continues to evolve, it will be essential to address regulatory, environmental, and technological challenges to unlock the full potential of this transformative technology.

The continued growth and adoption of cryptocurrencies will require collaboration between industry stakeholders, governments, and regulators. Clear and supportive regulatory frameworks can foster innovation while ensuring consumer protection and financial stability. Additionally, ongoing research and development efforts are needed to address scalability, security, and sustainability concerns, ensuring that cryptocurrencies can scale to meet the demands of a global economy.

Education and outreach efforts will also play a crucial role in promoting the responsible use of cryptocurrencies. By increasing digital literacy and awareness, individuals can make informed decisions and harness the benefits of this new financial landscape. As more people and businesses embrace cryptocurrencies, the collective knowledge and experience of the community will drive further innovation and growth.

In conclusion, cryptocurrencies have the potential to unshackle economies and create a more inclusive, efficient, and resilient global financial system. By leveraging the principles of decentralization, transparency, and security, cryptocurrencies can address the shortcomings of traditional financial systems and empower individuals and businesses around the world. As we embark on this journey, the blueprint for the future of global commerce is being drawn, and the possibilities are limitless.

Economies Unshackled: The Cryptocurrency Blueprint for Global Commerce

Embark on a riveting journey through the transformative world of cryptocurrencies and their profound impact on global commerce. "Economies Unshackled" delves into the origins, evolution, and potential of digital currencies to revolutionize traditional financial systems. From the pioneering days of Bitcoin to the rise of decentralized finance (DeFi) and central bank digital currencies (CBDCs), this book explores the key innovations that are reshaping the economic landscape.

Discover how blockchain technology serves as the backbone of cryptocurrencies, ensuring transparency, security, and immutability. Explore the rise of decentralized finance, which empowers individuals with unprecedented access to financial services, and the challenges and opportunities it presents. Uncover the environmental concerns associated with cryptocurrency mining and the sustainable solutions being developed to address them.

"Economies Unshackled" also examines the global regulatory landscape, the potential for financial inclusion, and the integration of cryptocurrencies into e-commerce. Learn how tokenization is creating new digital economies and the future of work is being redefined by decentralized platforms. As the world navigates this exciting frontier, the book provides a comprehensive blueprint for understanding and harnessing the power of cryptocurrencies to create a more inclusive, efficient, and resilient global financial system.

With insightful analysis and real-world examples, "Economies Unshackled" is an essential guide for anyone looking to understand the transformative potential of cryptocurrencies and their role in shaping the future of global commerce.

www.ingramcontent.com/pod-product-compliance
Lightning Source LLC
LaVergne TN
LVHW020741090526
838202LV00057BA/6172